# GOOD HOUSEKE
# RECIPE
## NOTEBOOK

Normal healthy appetites satisfied by good things to eat from your baker
*Fresh every day*
GOLD MEDAL FLOUR
*used by the best bakers everywhere*

WASHBURN'S *Eventually* GOLD MEDAL FLOUR Why Not Now?

EBURY PRESS STATIONERY

Published in 1993 by Ebury Press Stationery
An imprint of Random House UK Ltd
Random House, 20 Vauxhall Bridge Road
London SW1V 2SA

Copyright © Random House UK Ltd 1993

All rights reserved. No part of this book may be
reproduced in any form or by any means without
permission in writing from the publisher.

Set in Horley Old Style
By FMT Limited, London SE1

Printed in Hong Kong

Designed by Polly Dawes

ISBN 0 09 177460 8

Illustrations: page 1 "Washburn's Gold Medal Flour", poster
by René Clark 1925; page 7 "Post Toasties", 1916; page 15
"Grape-Nuts", 1913; page 27 "Royal Baking Powder", c. 1924;
page 39 "Jell-o", c. 1921; page 53 "Goodall's Products", 1920;
page 65 "Hovis Bread", 1923 from The Mary Evans Picture Library;
Cover illustration and page 73 courtesy Good Housekeeping
Magazine, National Magazine Company

# INTRODUCTION

This Recipe Collection Notebook is ideal for keeping your favourite Good Housekeeping recipes at your fingertips. Simply stick them – or write them – under the relevant headings: Breakfasts, Family Meals, Dinner Parties, and so on. There's even a Contents page so you can keep track of the recipes you add. And with the Index, you can build up a record of which cookery books contain the recipes you use most often. Again, for easy reference, it's divided into meal headings so you don't have to waste time leafing through piles of cookery books to find a specific recipe.

This Notebook is ideal for any cook who collects recipes – and who can resist doing so? It's so easy to use, you'll find all your favourite recipes in minutes.

Good cooking!

Moyra Fraser

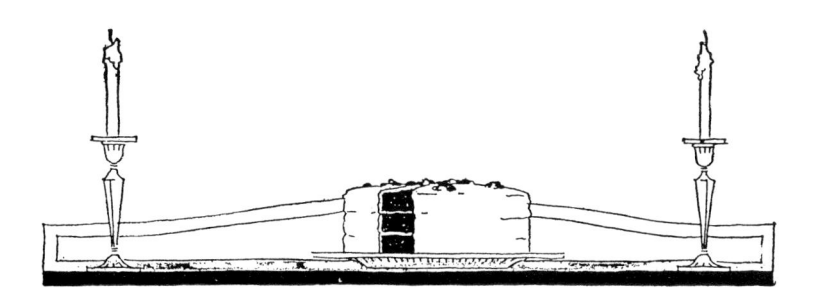

# Contents

| Recipe | Page Nº |
|---|---|
|  |  |

# Contents

| Recipe | Page Nº |
|--------|---------|
|        |         |

# Contents

| Recipe | Page Nº |
|---|---|
|  |  |

# BREAKFAST / BRUNCH

THE HOLD-UP

## NEW POST TOASTIES

Crisp—Delicious—The Perfect Corn Flakes

Copyright, 1916, Postum Cereal Co., Ltd.

# Breakfast / Brunch

# Breakfast / Brunch

## Comments

# Breakfast / Brunch

# Breakfast / Brunch

## Comments

# Breakfast / Brunch

# Breakfast / Brunch

**Comments**

# Breakfast / Brunch

# LUNCH

## Fresh Air and Natural Food

The most "natural" foods are the cereals.

These should be cooked at the factory in a clean and scientific manner to make them easily digestible.

## Grape=Nuts
### FOOD

Is made of wheat and barley, the greatest of all cereals, containing the tissue-building (proteids), energy-making (carbohydrates) elements; and *also* the "vital" phosphates (grown in the grains) which Nature requires for replacing the soft gray material of brain and nerve centres, worn away by Life's daily activities.

Follow the law of Old Mother Nature — eat Grape-Nuts and cream, and *give it to the children*, at least once a day.

*"There's a Reason"*

# Lunch

# Lunch

## Comments

# Lunch

# Lunch

## Comments

# Lunch

# Lunch

## Comments

# Lunch

# Lunch

## Comments

# Lunch

# Lunch

## Comments

# Lunch

# AFTERNOON TEA

# Afternoon Tea

# Afternoon Tea

## Comments

# Afternoon Tea

# Afternoon Tea

## Comments

# Afternoon Tea

# Afternoon Tea

| Comments |
|---|
|  |

# Family Meals

# Family Meals

## Comments

# Afternoon Tea

# Afternoon Tea

## Comments

# Afternoon Tea

# FAMILY MEALS

DOROTHY is five years old to-day. As usual on such occasions mamma has made up a big Cherry Jell-O dessert, and while Nan brings it on and serves it, cousin Betty and Peg congratulate each other on their good fortune. Bobbie's gleeful face expresses his sentiments, and Dorothy, with her arm about him, is happy.

For little party affairs, and for big ones,

## JELL-O

has come to be regarded as almost indispensable. So many different dishes—entrees and salads as well as desserts—can be made of it that the first consideration is: "What shall we serve in Jell-O?"

The new Jell-O Book, just out, is more beautiful and complete than any other ever issued, and it will be sent free to any woman furnishing her name and address.

There are six pure fruit flavors of Jell-O: Strawberry, Raspberry, Lemon, Orange, Cherry, Chocolate.

THE GENESEE PURE FOOD COMPANY
Le Roy, N. Y., and Bridgeburg, Ont.

# Family Meals

# FAMILY MEALS

## COMMENTS

# Family Meals

# Family Meals

## Comments

# Family Meals

# Family Meals

## Comments

# Family Meals

# Family Meals

Comments

# Family Meals

# Family Meals

## Comments

# Family Meals

# Family Meals

## Comments

# Family Meals

# DINNER PARTIES

## The Success of the Party

### GOODALL'S JELLY CRYSTALS

You can make the most perfect jellies—jellies with the famous Goodall real-fruit flavour—jellies chock full of deliciousness—from Goodall's Jelly Crystals. Moreover, such jellies are absolutely pure and cannot possibly harm anyone. Because each little crystal is in itself complete, you cannot get a patchy flavour with Goodall's Jelly Crystals.

*Pint packets 9d. from your Grocer.*

### GOODALL'S EGG POWDER

And now for the cakes—you *must* have plenty of dainty little cakes or shortbreads to hand round. They are so expensive to buy—yet so much nicer and cheaper if made at home with Goodall's Egg Powder that you can easily have a plentiful supply. Goodall's Egg Powder makes cakes, pastry, etc., as light, delicious and wholesome as if you had used the finest new-laid eggs.

*Large packets 1½d. Tins 5d. and 1/4.*

MAKE this year's party a *real* peace party—plenty of fun and merriment—but be sure there are plenty of goodies to eat, for success almost entirely depends upon the variety and daintiness of the refreshments. And in spite of peace-time prices it need not be a costly matter to make lots of lovely delicacies if you make them at home with Goodall's famous culinary aids.

Three generations of British housewives have learned the real meaning behind the name of "Goodall, Backhouse." Experience has taught them that wherever the name of this fine old Yorkshire firm appears it stands for purity, for wholesomeness, for good, honest value — for quality. That is why success is assured if you make a point of using Goodall's products.

### GOODALL, BACKHOUSE & Co., LEEDS
*Sole proprietors of Yorkshire Relish*

### GOODALL'S CUSTARD POWDER

Custard is always a popular feature—and Goodall's gives the best results. Its delicious rich creamy flavour makes Goodall's always a favourite. The children revel in it; and even the grown-ups are apt to ask for more—so be prepared. It is the simplest thing in the world to make if you insist on using Goodall's.

*Packets 7½d., & 1/3 and in large tins.*

### Yorkshire Relish

Sandwiches are another important item. Ham, chicken, beef or any meat or paste sandwiches are greatly improved by a light sprinkle of "The Most Delicious Sauce In The World"—Yorkshire Relish. This sauce is delightful with almost every kind of meat, fish or fowl, hot or cold. Try it!

*10½d., 1/9 & 3/6 per bottle from your Grocer.*

### RETURN YOUR BOTTLES.

Your Grocer will gladly pay you 1d. for each empty Yorkshire Relish bottle you return. Take them to your Grocer to-day and turn them into money.

# Dinner Parties

# Dinner Parties

## Comments

# Dinner Parties

# Dinner Parties

## Comments

# Dinner Parties

# Dinner Parties

## Comments

# Dinner Parties

# Dinner Parties

## Comments

# Dinner Parties

# Dinner Parties

## Comments

# Dinner Parties

### Comments

# PRESERVES / JAMS

*for grandma too!*

## She knows it's best for both

GRANNIE smiles approvingly at the little one. She knows that HOVIS is good for everybody—herself included. Little Dot loves it. Dad says it agrees with his digestion, whilst Mother finds it *so* sustaining.

# HOVIS
(Trade Mark)

is enriched with the golden germ of wheat—without the indigestible branny parts. That is where it gets its crisp, appetising flavour, its dainty appearance, its superb qualities of nourishment and easy digestion.

**Your Baker Bakes it**

HOVIS LTD., MACCLESFIELD

# Preserves / Jams

# Preserves / Jams

## Comments

# Preserves / Jams

# Preserves / Jams

## Comments

# Preserves / Jams

# Preserves / Jams

## Comments

# Preserves / Jams

## Comments

# INDEX

| Index | Breakfast / Brunch | |
|---|---|---|
| Recipe | Comments | Source & Page N° |
| | | |

| Index | Breakfast / Brunch | |
|---|---|---|
| Recipe | Comments | Source & Page Nº |
| | | |

| Index | Breakfast / Brunch | |
|---|---|---|
| Recipe | Comments | Source & Page Nº |
| | | |

| Index Recipe | Lunch Comments | Source & Page Nº |
|---|---|---|
| | | |

| INDEX | LUNCH | |
|---|---|---|
| RECIPE | COMMENTS | SOURCE & PAGE Nº |
| | | |

| Index | Lunch | |
|---|---|---|
| Recipe | Comments | Source & Page N° |

| Index | Lunch | |
|---|---|---|
| Recipe | Comments | Source & Page Nº |
| | | |

| Index | Lunch | |
|---|---|---|
| Recipe | Comments | Source & Page Nº |

# Index

## Afternoon Tea

| Recipe | Comments | Source & Page Nº |
|--------|----------|------------------|
|        |          |                  |

| Recipe | Comments | Source & Page Nº |
|---|---|---|
| | | |

| Index | Afternoon Tea | |
|---|---|---|
| Recipe | Comments | Source & Page Nº |
| | | |

| Index | Afternoon Tea | |
|---|---|---|
| Recipe | Comments | Source & Page Nº |

| Index | Family Meals | |
|---|---|---|
| Recipe | Comments | Source & Page Nº |
| | | |

| INDEX | FAMILY MEALS | |
|---|---|---|
| RECIPE | COMMENTS | SOURCE & PAGE Nº |
| | | |
| | | |
| | | |
| | | |
| | | |
| | | |
| | | |
| | | |
| | | |
| | | |
| | | |
| | | |
| | | |
| | | |
| | | |
| | | |
| | | |
| | | |
| | | |
| | | |
| | | |
| | | |
| | | |
| | | |
| | | |
| | | |
| | | |
| | | |
| | | |
| | | |
| | | |

# Index

## Family Meals

| Recipe | Comments | Source & Page Nº |
|--------|----------|------------------|
|        |          |                  |

| Index | Family Meals | |
|---|---|---|
| Recipe | Comments | Source & Page Nº |
| | | |

| Index | Dinner Parties | |
|---|---|---|
| Recipe | Comments | Source & Page Nº |
| | | |

| Index | Dinner Parties | |
|---|---|---|
| Recipe | Comments | Source & Page Nº |
| | | |

| Index | Dinner Parties | |
|---|---|---|
| RECIPE | COMMENTS | SOURCE & PAGE Nº |
| | | |

| INDEX | DINNER PARTIES | |
|---|---|---|
| RECIPE | COMMENTS | SOURCE & PAGE Nº |
| | | |

# Index — Preserves / Jams

| Recipe | Comments | Source & Page Nº |
|--------|----------|------------------|
|        |          |                  |

| INDEX | PRESERVES / JAMS | |
|---|---|---|
| RECIPE | COMMENTS | SOURCE & PAGE Nº |
| | | |

| INDEX | PRESERVES / JAMS | |
|---|---|---|
| RECIPE | COMMENTS | SOURCE & PAGE Nº |
| | | |